CRAYOLA
HALLOWEEN
COLORS

ROBIN NELSON

LERNER PUBLICATIONS ◆ MINNEAPOLIS

Official Licensed Product
Lerner Publications Company
A division of Lerner Publishing Group, Inc.
241 First Avenue North
Minneapolis, MN 55401 USA

For reading levels and more information, look up this title at www.lernerbooks.com.

Main body text set in Billy Infant Regular 24/30.
Typeface provided by SparkyType.

Library of Congress Cataloging-in-Publication Data

Names: Nelson, Robin, 1971- author.
Title: Crayola® halloween colors / by Robin Nelson.
Description: Minneapolis : Lerner Publications, 2019. | Series: Crayola® holiday colors | Includes
    bibliographical references and index. | Audience: Age 4-9. | Audience: K to grade 3.
Identifiers: LCCN 2017048246 (print) | LCCN 2017056389 (ebook) | ISBN 9781541512450 (eb
    pdf) | ISBN 9781541510920 (lb : alk. paper) | ISBN 9781541527485 (pb : alk. paper)
Subjects: LCSH: Halloween—Juvenile literature. | Colors—Juvenile literature.
Classification: LCC GT4965 (ebook) | LCC GT4965 .N45 2018 (print) | DDC 394.2646—dc23

LC record available at https://lccn.loc.gov/2017048246

Manufactured in the United States of America
1-43976-33990-2/7/2018

TABLE OF CONTENTS

HALLOWEEN IS HERE!

What holiday is filled with pumpkins, fun costumes, and yummy candy?

It's Halloween!

Bright **ORANGE** pumpkins as far as the eye can see—which one will you choose?

Pumpkins are ready to harvest in the fall around Halloween.

HALLOWEEN DECORATIONS

A carved mouth, nose, and eyes turn a pumpkin into a jack-o'-lantern.

Some pumpkins are painted bright colors.

Pumpkins can be silly or scary!

WHITE webs make houses look haunted.

It's fun to decorate for Halloween!

Some people believe black cats bring bad luck.

Spiders and bats are around every corner.
Watch out for **BLACK** cats!

These children are celebrating Halloween with a party!

CELEBRATING HALLOWEEN

People dress up in their favorite costumes for Halloween.

Children go
house to house
collecting treats.

Bags, pillowcases, or pumpkin
carriers are filled with treats.

Trick or treat!

TREATS

There are so many yummy
things to eat on Halloween!

Candy, caramel apples, cupcakes, and more!

What is your favorite Halloween treat?

YELLOW, ORANGE, and **WHITE** candy corn is a special Halloween treat. Tiny **ORANGE** candy pumpkins are too!

WHITE ghosts, **PURPLE** bats, and **GREEN** witches.

There are lots of ways to decorate Halloween cookies. Yum!

Spooking friends with scary treats is fun!

Some treats are creepy!

People make monster snacks or edible fingers.

CREEPY COLORS

From glowing **YELLOW** eyes to oozing **GREEN** slime, Halloween is full of colors!

COPY AND COLOR!

Halloween is filled with haunting colors! Here are some of the Crayola® crayon colors used in this book. What colors will you use to celebrate? Copy these pages, and color the symbols of Halloween.

RED ORANGE

BLUE VIOLET

MANGO TANGO

YELLOW ORANGE

GRANNY SMITH APPLE

29

GLOSSARY

caramel: sticky brown candy

carved: cut out or into pieces

costumes: clothes to make you look different

decorate: to add color, design, or other features that improve the appearance of something

edible: able to be eaten

haunted: something believed to be visited or lived in by a ghost

TO LEARN MORE

BOOKS

Bullard, Lisa. *My Family Celebrates Halloween*. Illustrated by Holli Conger. Minneapolis: Lerner Publications, 2019. It's time for Hailey's favorite holiday—Halloween! Learn how Hailey celebrates with her family and friends.

Grabill, Rebecca. *Halloween Good Night*. New York: Atheneum Books for Young Readers, 2017. Read this Halloween bedtime story starring monsters you know and love.

Walker, Sally M. *Druscilla's Halloween*. Minneapolis: Carolrhoda Books, 2009. Read this fun story about the witch who first thought of flying on a broomstick.

WEBSITES

Creepy Spider Web Doorway
http://www.crayola.com/crafts/creepy-spider-web-doorway-craft/
Decorate your door for Halloween with this fun craft project.

Halloween Crafts and Children's Activities
http://www.dltk-holidays.com/halloween/
Celebrate Halloween with these crafts, coloring pages, worksheets, poems, songs, and other activities.

Halloween Facts for Kids
https://kidzfeed.com/halloween-facts-for-kids/
Visit this website to learn more fun facts about Halloween.

INDEX

PHOTO ACKNOWLEDGMENTS

The images in this book are used with the permission of: nicemosaic/Shutterstock.com, pp. 2, 30, 31, 32 (spiderweb background); Photos used with the permission of Rasta Imposta, p. 4; cmannphoto/iStock/Getty Images, p. 5 (top left); Juanmonino/E+/Getty Images, pp. 5 (top right), 20; Monkey Business Images/Shutterstock.com, p. 5 (bottom left); Arina P Habich/Shutterstock.com, p. 5 (bottom right); Image Source/Photodisc/Getty Images, p. 7; darak77/iStock/Getty Images, p. 8; mediaphotos/iStock/Getty Images, p. 9; voyta/iStock/Getty Images, pp. 10–11; crisserbug/iStock/Getty Images, p. 12; M_a_y_a/E+/Getty Images, p. 13; gpointstudio/Shutterstock.com, pp. 14–15; kali9/E+/Getty Images, pp. 16, 17; Natalia Wimberley/Shutterstock.com, p. 18; Elena Schweitzer/Shutterstock.com, pp. 19, 23; JeniFoto/Shutterstock.com, p. 21; mphillips007/iStock/Getty Images, p. 24; Elena Shashkina/Shutterstock.com, p. 25; poutmagazine/iStock/Getty Images, p. 26; Arina P Habich/Shutterstock.com, p. 27; © Laura Westlund/Independent Picture Service, pp. 28, 29 (illustrations).

Cover: Dan76/Shutterstock.com (girl); Arina P Habich/Shutterstock.com (candy); © James Baker/bestreviewsbase.com/flickr.com (CC BY 2.0) (trees); © William Warby/flickr.com (CC BY 2.0) (jack-o'-lanterns).